HILLS & VALLEYS

AND THE SPIRITUAL WARFARE IN BETWEEN

15-Day Interactive Study Guide

Reflective Questions for
Personal Development and Group Discussions

©2020 by Alma Fisher

All rights reserved. No part of this book may be reproduced in any form without permission in writing from the author, except in the case of brief quotations embodied in critical articles or reviews. AlmaFisher.Com

ISBN: 978-1-951614-12-6 (paperback)
Printed in the United States of America
almafisher.com

HILLS & VALLEYS

AND THE SPIRITUAL WARFARE IN BETWEEN

Alma Fisher

"FOR I KNOW THE THOUGHTS THAT I THINK TOWARD YOU, SAITH THE LORD, THOUGHTS OF PEACE, AND NOT OF EVIL, TO GIVE YOU AN EXPECTED END."

(JER. 29:11 KING JAMES VERSION)

FOREWARD

When I first heard of this book, my mind immediately went to the story in 1 Kings where King Ahab finds himself surrounded by his enemies for a second time. This enemy had already experienced defeat at the hand of God and came to the conclusion that it was all about the location they were fighting in. In pagan culture, their gods had territories, which is why they determined that the God of Israel was God over the hills. This is much like today, the god of this world has territories. They are set up all around us, in our neighborhoods, schools, markets, places of employment and the list can go on and on. As it was in the days of King Ahab, even in the midst of this wicked and perverse generation, we know that our God he is Lord of all.

Highs and Lows are a part of life, and as Christians, we sometimes feel the need to pray more when we are in the valley more than when we are on the mountaintop. Spiritual warfare is ongoing, it never stops. The Bible says we wrestle not against flesh and blood. Our enemy doesn't get tired! As you read this book, prepare your heart and ask God to open up your understanding to more of his Word. Examine your heart and see where change is needed then make the appropriate changes. No book can ever replace the Bible! Let this fifteen-day devotion be used as a guide to help you on your spiritual journey. After reading, go to the Bible and see what God is saying to you for yourself, for He does speak through his word! I pray that you finish this devotional with a deeper understanding of

God's word, love, and devotion toward you. Remember, He is Lord of all.

Ebony Lynnel Harris
BE Publishing Co.

LETTER FROM THE AUTHOR

Have you ever said "Why did this have to happen to me or how could something this terrible happen to my loved one?" If you have not verbalized this, you have more than likely thought it. This is what our humanity screams when we are stopped on the journey to fulfill our dreams. When troubles pour in like streams of water, and the money continually comes up shorter and shorter, then there are problems with your 13 or even 30-year-old daughter, and you feel borderline schizophrenic. Yes, all of these feelings are possible even while walking with Christ. However, they cannot overtake you unless you give into them.

This brings us to the theme scripture of this book which is: "For I know the thoughts that I think toward you, saith the LORD, thoughts of peace, and not of evil, to give you an expected end" (Jer. 29:11 King James Version). God desires for us to understand that we are his friends and that everything that He breaks, He mends. The end result depends on whether or not we yield to the process. The light affliction we endure in the valley only lasts for a moment, if we believe and receive this we will make it to another hill experience.

When you find yourself in the midst of a valley experience, you can decide to continue trusting God and persevere or you can veer off and find your own way. However, if you decide to go your own way I must warn you that your plans will fail. "There is a way which seemeth right unto a man, but the end thereof are the ways of death" (Prov. 14:12). Thus, it is better to accept God's will for your life and allow him to navigate you through the Hills and Valleys of it. I cannot say that all of your life will be full of joy; neither can I say it will be full of sadness, but the word of God declares, "they that suffer with him will also reign with Him." (2 Tim. 2:12a). This is God's promise to you if you continue with Him.

This book was inspired by the many hardships that I have faced throughout my spiritual journey, it consists of 15 poems. Each poem has a devotional with 2 questions which together are designed to provide an explanation for each piece and offer guidance.

I pray that you increase in knowledge and become more committed to God after going through this devotional.

Author Alma Fisher

Alma Fisher

TABLE OF CONTENTS

Foreward 5

Letter From the Author 7

Table of Contents 9

Highs & Lows 11

Genetics 17

Spiritual Maturity 25

Resurrection 33

Prove Me 41

Pain 49

Peace 55

Miss You 63

Destroying The Yokes 71

I Will Praise Him 79

Failure 85

Women 91

Fly 97

Package 103

Fire Within 109

List of Sponsors 115

DAY 1
HIGHS & LOWS

Seems I've had more cons than pros.
Seems like the rain doesn't pour enough for my grass to grow.
Yes, an intermittent shine,
in exchange for an unrelenting grind.
But it's all creating a unique line to get me there on time.
Yes, to my destination.
See, it's so complex that I can't make all of this rhyme.
Hopefully, this book piece by piece will give you an inkling of how these failures and victories shifted my trajectory.
As the ink leaks from my pen, I hope that it will inspire someone to flee from sin and reposition them to win. Shall we begin?

DEVOTION

To everything that happens under the sun there is a season. Sometimes we think of things as if they are super complicated, when it could just be your season to suffer. Each season of life is mentioned in Ecclesiastes 3 and mourning is one of them, but so is laughter. One must keep in mind that every season must change and as each one is mandated to change so are we. As human beings and especially as believers we must grow and develop. We can develop by praying, fasting, attending church and connecting with strong fellow Christians. By connecting with other strong believers we establish a lifeline to draw strength from during difficult storms. The enemy is a deceiver, so he works strategically to make you believe that your current valley is your final fate, but God has great things in store for you.

The Devil is confined within the four walls of a season, thus, the temptation cannot go beyond the season. When you are at your lowest point in the deepest pit of the valley, you have yet to embark on your highs in Christ. Though the valley experience is undesirable, it works cohesively with the hill experience to produce our expected end.

QUESTIONS TO PONDER

1. What season are you currently in? Using the above devotional what can you do during this season that will better prepare you for your next season?

    Example: If you are waiting on a supervisory promotion, you can start by studying people management skills and taking leadership training courses.

2. Did the above devotional change your perspective on your current season or seasons in general?

    If so, write down how and how you can better embrace future seasons.

DAY 2
GENETICS

My ability to manipulate phonetics is in my genetics; it's kind of like those synthetic fibers that us African Americans put together and make hairstyles like we're multiple MacGyvers.
He could take a peanut from a star and make an entire prenuptial agreement.
He was incredible, not in strength, but in genius.
His wit could match the combined talent of Venus and Serena's.
What am I saying to you?
What is that thing you do that while doing it you are less stressed?
What is that thing you do with ease that would take others years to process?
Whatever it is, don't digress, move forward with it and progress.
Use your God-given talents to help change someone's life.
Though you may be shy, you are called to help somebody.
So don't dim down the jewels on your crown to pretend that your feet are planted firmly on the ground with everybody else's. For, that would be absolutely selfish.
Not everyone's gift is singing, dancing, or preaching.
A great gift is reaching!
Yes, your ability to effectively communicate.

That doesn't mean that your diction has to be great.
It means that you have to be able to relate to others.
So, work to uncover your gifts and as Jesus said:
"freely ye have received, freely give."

DEVOTION

Most people desire to have gifts and abilities that would leave the listener or beholder in awe. However, every single thing that God does is purposeful and not everyone's purpose is to be a singer, dancer, or preacher. Although everyone's gifts are not those that were previously mentioned, everyone who has been baptized of the water and Spirit has the ability to reach someone. It is God's will for us to sow seeds and to meet the needs of others and guide them to Christ. A great witness is our life, but we must go even further than that. Our responsibility as Christians is to tell the world about the gospel of Jesus Christ. This is what is referred to as *the great commission* which is indicated in: (Matt. 28:16-20). This is imperative because it is a requirement for one to make it into the kingdom of heaven. "Then Peter said unto them, Repent, and be baptized every one of you in the name of Jesus Christ for the remission of sins, and ye shall receive the gift of the Holy Ghost" (Acts 2:38). So, use your voice on social media or whenever there is an opportunity to spread the gospel of Jesus Christ.

A large part of the dissatisfaction with our individual talents is our lack of contentment and understanding of who we are in God. The scripture indicates that: "godliness with contentment is great gain" (1 Tim. 6:6). Therefore, we should not be striving to be on stage, if our position is behind the scenes making sure that the show runs smoothly. It would be out of order for the person who opens and closes the curtains to get on stage and begin acting. In fact, it would disrupt the show. This would look just as ridiculous as it sounds.

Yes, singing, dancing, and preaching are glorious gifts, but they are not where every part of the body fits. Could you imagine where the church would be if those were the only functions of the body? The church could not survive, but God who is omniscient understood this way before He created us. Therefore, we should trust him and fulfill our portion with gladness.

Contentment can be gained by seeking God and studying to learn more of Him and also seeking out and learning more about the talents that we possess to find our purpose.

QUESTIONS TO PONDER

1. Are you content with your calling in God? Do you know what your calling is?

If not, use this devotion and write journal entries on ways seek God for clarity on your purpose in Christ.

2. Are you jealous over other people's gifts?

If so, start with meditating on the following scripture:" but godliness with contentment is great gain" (Tim. 6:6).

DAY 3
SPIRITUAL MATURITY

We must reach the place of spiritual maturity to activate our authority.
We must leave from spiritual insecurity
and realize that God surely can.
We must understand that, if God said that He is for me then surely the enemy cannot destroy me.

We must stay and pray even when we don't realize that God is there.
We must stay strong even in front of the enemies glare and
take the time to properly prepare.
You see we got too much time for gossip,
but not enough time to build up our spiritual biceps and triceps.
We are frustrated because we are not progressing as much as we should, but God is only going to feed you more
food, after you've finished digesting what He's already given you.
But we are not ready because we are still too busy being petty and we are not ready because we are still as slippery as spaghetti, so you are not able to put our name on that next label or to put our book on that next table.
Because we are diligent in being unstable.

Because we are busy watching cable, Netflix, Fire Sticks, but not Pure Flix. So, we are in a constant state of spiritual trepidation because we are carnally motivated.
Forgetting that the pleasures of sin are overrated.
Meditating on the wrong things like, "they are hating."

They are not hating, they are earnestly waiting to see the manifestation, but it's difficult to see through so much spiritual stagnation.

While we are waiting, so are all the nations, because we are called to reach the nations, called to preach salvation, called not to be eager, but to be patient with those who do not understand this walk. So, we must watch the way we walk and the way we talk because God said with love and kindness have I drawn you not with the mentality that I must be addressed as your highness.

We must be careful because it can be the finest little thing that can stop us from being able to shine this little thing.
So, we must make sure that our walk is lined up with what we sing and that we are not just shaking a tambourine while slipping into spiritual atrophy.

So that we are growing so spiritually strong that with our prayers we can block catastrophe.
We need to be in a place where the enemy is alarmed because we are armed and are no longer charmed by his snare,
but are ahead of his tactics and are quicker because we have visualized where he was before he got there.

Yes, the opening of our spiritual eyes being the prize for our refusal to compromise and mix God's stuff with the Devil's stuff. Because God's more than enough.

For lightness and darkness do not mix, which is why my eyes are fixed on the crucifix that God released his life upon, which is the ground I shall stand upon. The unshakable, forever bond, Who inspired the rock the church was built upon to say, "repent, and be baptized every one of you in the name of Jesus Christ for the remission of sins, and ye shall receive the gift of the Holy Ghost." So, I can boast in the one who innocently gave up The Ghost. I will spread the gospel from coast to coast, since it is no surprise that the time is getting close. Not everyone's exit will be greeted by a heavenly host. So, we must give the more earnest heed and work to succeed by showing that love is a deed and provide the bandage for those who bleed. We must reach the place of spiritual maturity so we can fully operate in our authority.

DEVOTION

It is important for Christians to not remain at a baby stage in Christ, but to go on to maturity. This is a must if we are going to make it to Heaven. The body of Christ has to measure up to the full stature of God. God does not expect or require for us to reach this level overnight, but He does give an allotted time for this process.

As Paul indicated: " When I was a child I spake as a child, but when I became a man I put away childish things" (1 Cor. 13:11). As God leads and instructs us, we must continually progress and grow spiritually "while it is still day: the night cometh when no man can work" (John 9:4 a). If we do not leave the baby stage, we cannot finish our work. We will be unproductive servants because we have not graduated to the expected height. Again, the Christian believer must progress in order to lead and help the unsaved, non-believers, and newborn babes in Christ. Putting forth effort into being a good steward over what God has entrusted in us is a way of honoring him. The Bible instructs us to add to our faith. See: 2 Pet. 1:5. By adding to our faith, we are giving God a return on his investment and as aforementioned God expects productivity. On more than one occasion, in the Bible, God cut down and punished the unproductive things and or person(s). In the book of Luke, we see this act carried out on the tree that was unfruitful and on the servant who hid his talents in the book of Matthew. These accounts can be found in Luke 13:7 and Matthew 25:24-28, respectively. A lack of productivity is wicked and wickedness is an exact opposite of

God's character. In the beginning, God exemplified his beliefs of working through creating, producing, adding and helping his creation.

Just as children display the characteristics of their parents, we as Christians should manifest the attributes of our heavenly father. The Bible declares, " If the righteous scarcely make it in where shall the sinner and ungodly appear" (1 Pet. 4:18). Therefore, we must adhere to the word of God and mature so that we can hear, "well done thou good and faithful servant" (Matt. 25:21).

QUESTIONS TO PONDER

1. Have you added to your faith, since you have been saved?

   If the answer to this question is not one that you are satisfied with, what can you do to change this? If the answer is one that you and an accountability partner would be proud of, continue on this path.

2. Having a spiritual mentor is important for your growth. This person should be someone who is godly and already spiritually mature. Do you have a spiritual mentor?

DAY 4
RESURRECTION

I don't feel inspired, but what I do feel is tired.
I'm not complaining. I'm just explaining how I allowed myself to get depressed, slipped up and regressed, so the enemy has been able to suppress my gift.
Yes, that was it!
He wanted to stop it from flowing.
He wanted to stop me from growing, all the while I was knowing his tactics.
I just sat back and allowed him to haggle me into thinking on my misery, while he left with parts of me.
Some of which I didn't know was gone, until I tried to sing my song and all that came out was an exasperated yawn.

Yes, due to the quiet devastation that took place in my head; and the residue manifests in the way that I mistreat you. Yes, the residue manifests in the way that I misconstrue almost everything you do.
I allowed the author of confusion to present me an optical illusion. Rather than rebuke him for his intrusion, I offered him a seat of his choosing. See, I was abusing my privilege as a steward over this

mind. For, I thought I had the space and time for neglect only to end up deeply in debt because I had not kept my mind on thee.

If I had, I wouldn't be standing here gasping for peace, while the devil is laughing at me. No, this didn't have to be because I know the ropes, yet the enemy keeps trapping me.

Yes, I allowed him to hang me by allowing him to resurface everything that ever pained me. Though countless times you trained me on how to defeat the devil so much so that I should be able to do so even in my sleep.

Lord, there needs to be a resurrection, a resurrection of your reflection!

A people who are no longer stumbling at the forewarned rejection, but people who are earnestly striving toward perfection.

Yes, people who are willing to take an examination of the damnation that we have caused to our own souls. People who are willing to leave off their own agenda and return to the goal, which is the goal of the saving of souls.

Then maybe we'd perform those signs and wonders to the magnitude that you said we do.

We don't need another person with just something to say, no we need an actual paved out way.

That way has already been given, for Jesus is the way, the truth and the light and His word will cut out everything that's not right.

We just have to be willing to be a light and we can start this night by making it our resurrection.

DEVOTION

A resurrection can come about by drawing closer to God and by increasing our communion with Him. Prayer is essential for one to be a strong child of God. Therefore, it is imperative that we are intentional about our prayer lives. God instructs us to draw nigh to him and He will draw nigh to us. We draw closer to God by seeking him out. There are multiple ways that we can seek God. A couple of methods are by frequently attending church services and taking courses for the furthering of our spiritual education. These things are not a substitution for prayer, but are other methods of getting to know the Lord better.

If our dilemma is a busy schedule, we need to incorporate a prayer time into the busy schedule. Yes, prayer should be one of those things on our to-do list. We can intentionally pray for 15 minute segments twice-daily and can later increase this time from 15 to 30 minutes twice-daily. We must also read the word in order to cleanse ourselves from all filthiness of the spirit and of the flesh. Thus, we have to do some work even after we receive salvation by losing weight spiritually. After we lose this weight, we must keep it off by maintaining a spiritual regiment. There are levels in our walk with Christ, for we go from faith to faith, and from glory to glory. God may require you to pray more, if you stay in communion with him, He will let you know what He requires of you. This quality time with God will increase your spiritual growth. It is also important to seek God's perfect will for your life and through this He will reveal His assignments for your life. Every Christian's assignment is to go into the world compelling dying men and women to be saved. If you are intimidated, you can ask God for boldness and He will lead you and direct you.

QUESTIONS TO PONDER

1. How is your prayer life? Do you struggle with making time for God? If you are not struggling with your prayer life, using the above devotional how can you avail more of yourself to the Lord? If you struggle with this, work on being intentional about your time and you can even seek out a spiritual friend who will hold you accountable for this.

2. Are you faithful in your church attendance? If not, write out some things that can be removed off of your to-do list in order to fit more church services in. You can also see about adjusting some parts of your schedule to make more time for God. If this is an option, consider going into work early so that you can leave earlier.

DAY 5

PROVE ME

I was at the place in my life where the clouds rolled up their sleeves and flared up their nostrils, and blew a sneeze that violently ripped through the trees.

Smacking the leaves so hard that they froze in mid-air before falling to the ground, where they found their final resting place.
Yes, this place was seemingly devoid of God's grace, but clearly, it was laced with his presence because I'm still running this race.

Yes, I stood face to face with the storm that was so powerful that it caused me to transform.
It was so close that I could taste the intensity of the heat as it clasped my face and began to erase any trace of any former disgraced areas and of wasted space.

Yes, instead of the fire disfiguring me it worked like a computer app and started reconfiguring me, made me more quip to handle new blessings.
See, God molded me through a multiplicity of lessons.

It made my system more sophisticated, so that I could be worthy to be elevated.
Yes, it made me stand out and actually be the person whom I was created to be.

No, this affliction wasn't because God hated me, but it was because He was taking me higher and making me birth the blessings through the fire. The heat forced me to come up out of the mess that I was in. Yes, but some areas of my life were just not right!

It didn't happen when I least expected, but when I felt the most rejected.
When I felt least respected.
When I thought my feet would begin to tell the story of how they fell.
Because I was tempted to say "oh well".
It was then that you proved me.

Your allowance of frustration and the confusion threatening to consume me was just to groom me.
The nightmare would soon be over, but it wasn't until I spiritually grew older that I could see what you saw all along, over my shoulder.

Now with this knowledge, I'm getting bolder, since you lifted the boulder off of my shoulder.

Now I can display the characteristics of a true soldier, and help somebody else climb over the hurdle because I understand the importance of girding up the loins of one's mind.

Now I don't have to be running afraid, but I can be at peace with the understanding that the price has already been paid.
I can save my pennies that were being squandered on my little mini tantrums.

Yes, and leave off poor little me and dance because God gave me the victory. My salvation is no longer a mystery, but is a vacation that I will be going on indefinitely.

DEVOTION

Sometimes as Christian believers, we do not understand why our tests or trials are so intense and this can be intimidating. However, it is important to keep in mind that pressure pushes us to levels that we would not otherwise reach. As a mother has to experience great pressure during the delivery of her baby, so does a Christian in order for him or her to grow in Christ. This is also the same as other natural experiences. The army, navy, and marines utilize this same tactic to transform civilians into soldiers. If you have fallen into sin, you do not have to stay there. The Bible says, "If we confess our sins, he is faithful and just to forgive us our sins, and to cleanse us from all unrighteousness" (1 John 1:9). Otherwise, when God turns up the heat it is to burn stuff off that is not like Him. Therefore, a child of God can have peace during this time for it is to help make him or her more pleasing to God.

QUESTIONS TO PONDER

1. What circumstances are you currently facing in your Christian walk?

2. If you are in a season of peace, how can you use your knowledge from prior experiences to help a brother or sister who may be dealing with this issue?

DAY 6
PAIN

Here's the story of my life
pain, rain, pain, strain, pressure.
A hand holding out a small gesture of deliverance
only being closed up by a false alarm.
Then it starts all over again.
Here's the story of my life,
but what I had to do was retrain my mind to see the beauty in the pain.
When I looked back again, I could see your glory in my life.

DEVOTION

P ain is something that most people hate to feel. It is often the reason why some people shut down after being hurt by someone. Despite how innate the act of shutting down in response to pain may seem, pain, in general, is necessary for growth. Likewise, it is necessary for Christian believers to develop. So, we cannot shy away from the test for relief. If we hold on we will see the glory of God unfold out of our painful situation.

QUESTIONS TO PONDER

1. Do you seem to be in a constant state of pain? Can you find purpose in your afflictions?

2. Can you see how your tests and trials have blessed your life? If so, write down the different ways in which your afflictions have enriched your life. If not, utilize this devotion as a guideline to shift your perspective of your tests and trials.

DAY 7
PEACE

Stop worrying about who did and didn't invite you and who does and doesn't like you and work on you liking you.

You must realize it is the enemy who is fighting you.
He's been heightening your senses by making you believe that God is not a God who recompenses.
Take down those emotional fences for these barriers are too expensive.
They are causing you massive destruction because you rather believe the enemies manipulations rather than God's instructions.

As a man thinketh so is he. You keep seeing yourself as a mustard seed, instead of standing up triumphantly.
Consequently, up until this point, you've been failing miserably, but today I came to speak of victory!

Yes, your days of saying that your giants are insurmountable are history. If you rehearse His word, instead of your misery and stop spewing out doubt, you'll start soaring above the high thing that exalts itself against the knowledge of God.

See, this isn't even one of those problems where you have to think hard, give it to God.

He said that in the last days I would pour out my spirit among all flesh, but He also said that men would become lovers of themselves.

Thus we see so many naked idols on these shelves, in the stores, even behind closed doors.
When we are minding our business and cleaning our floors we have to see somebody on TV prancing around in their draws.

Flesh is nasty and people want to do away with anything remotely close to classy.
So, I will pray and believe that you will not pass me by and wait on You, for, You are not a man that ye shall lie.
Don't worry if you're in a season that's dry. He that shall come will come and He will not tarry.

DEVOTION

The Bible says, "we walk by faith, and not by sight" (2 Cor. 5:7). This scripture indicates that we will not base our lives solely off of what we see, but off of God's word.

God gives us instructions at times that are the opposite of what men may expect from us. No matter how peculiar the instructions may seem, we must obey God. Sometimes God leads us to change our direction, we may not understand this, but God does. He is the God who was, is, and is yet to come. Therefore, it is wise to obey His instructions.

On one occasion there was a delay with the train that I would usually take in the evening and this led me to take another route. While I was on the bus, God instructed me to pray. It was only myself, the bus driver and one other passenger on the bus. Shortly thereafter, the bus driver was almost involved in a collision. I believe that God placed me there to intercede on their behalf. The outcome of the situation could have resulted in the death of the driver, passenger, and operator of the other vehicle.

This is just one illustration of how extremely important it is for us to walk by faith and allow God to direct our steps. For, someone's life is predicated upon our obedience to God. This is true whether we believe it or not! Finally, God knows the way, so if He tells us not to worry we do not have to worry. This is easier said than done, but

God desires for us to trust Him. If we cannot trust Him, we will not be able to endure until the end. So, we must trust our omnipresent and omniscient God. It is only through Him that we can obtain what has not yet materialized and in this we can have peace.

QUESTIONS TO PONDER

1. Are you struggling to obey God's voice for fear of what you do or do not see? If so, how can you apply this devotional to build up your faith in Christ?

2. If you are not struggling, how can you mentor and help others to increase their faith?

DAY 8

MISS YOU

I miss you.
Lately, this has been a recurring issue.
When it happens, I just have to pick up my tissues and decorate them with the saddest designs.
There are multiple lines and some parts where the colors are so dark, I can't tell them apart.

It starts with one drop and it turns into a showering of colors, some light, but they just get swallowed up in the others.
The others are usually more dominant because the stain from the pain of your absence is yet prominent.
However, you are now free and this is a relief from my grief,
that you are free.

For often you and I would sit back and share chuckles, while we watched and buckled our seatbelts and anticipated the impact that the people on the screen were unaware that they were about to feel.

I remember how you kneeled and cried for your mother because that was a wound that would just not completely heal.
See, there is no pill that could take away this ill feeling.

No, I won't stand here and fake it and say every day you will feel like you can make it, but I will be emotionally naked and tell you that some days you will feel absolutely vacant and impatient for the depth of the pain to ease.

Though time helps us cope with the pain,
there is no magical soap that can totally erase these scars.
I guess it's just too far for it to reach or is it just that God is so awesomely deep, He created a bond that could never be completely severed. He is the epitome of cleverness.

Even though you're not here, sometimes it's like we're still together. At times when I speak, I am in disbelief because it's as if you've entered the room. Sometimes I expect your call, then I remember.

The purpose of this poem is not to cast one down, it is to open one up so you can understand that though you have lost a loved one you can still carry on.

Now the grieving process varies on an individual level.
So, it's okay to take a tour of sadness.
Yes, it's okay to visit there,
just as long as we don't stay there,
and decay there, but pray there.

God will meet you there,
for He is a very present help in the time of trouble.
Yes, He will come to get you up out of the rubble
in your mind and help you.

If you are walking with Him,
one day, God will wipe away all of your tears.
It doesn't matter if you've grieved for years,
if you are one of His children, it is His business to deliver you.

He is not a respecter of people.
He said come unto me, all ye that labor and are heavy laden, and I will give you rest.
So, I would suggest that you give God a try.
If you are walking with him, don't worry, He will give you rest.

DEVOTION

As odd as it seems, grief is a normal thing. It is something that every human being will more than likely be affected by. Nevertheless, the knowledge of this thing does not make it easier to handle. An important thing that you must know when a season of grief is upon you is that there is hope.

The enemy does not want you to know that there will be better days. He wants you to believe that this is not just a season, but remember the Bible informed us that, "to everything, there is a season" (Ecc. 3:1a). You will not always be in deep depression; you will laugh again.

You can talk to God about all of your problems, and if you feel you need to speak to someone seek godly counsel. You can search for that in your church leadership such as your pastor or in licensed Christian mental health counselors. God has provided "everything we need pertaining to life and godliness" (2 Peter 1:3). This includes mental health counselors. If you are in deep grief, be encouraged and seek God for instruction and He will answer you.

QUESTIONS TO PONDER

1. Are you in the process of grieving a loved one? If you have not directly lost someone, do you know someone who is currently in grief? If so, using the above devotional write out some different avenues that you or they can take to assist with healing.

2. Do you have a support system? Are you trying to funnel through the ups and downs of this trying time alone? If you are, write down some names of positive, discreet people who you can vent to and reach out to them.

DAY 9

DESTROYING THE YOKES

I must train my heart to heal, train my mind to not entertain everything that wants to leave in imprinted stain.
Refrain from stalking the thoughts that have me parking my destiny in the middle of nowhere by focusing on someone who doesn't at all care for me.

Someone who could care less about me, someone who walks past me and does not even notice me.
Someone who sleeps peacefully, while I eat grudgingly because inwardly they are bugging me.

No, I have to stop drugging me with these fantasies and be candid and see that it's not at all about me.
And let go of all the ungodly visions, ungodly decisions because of the enemies incisions of implanted hate.

Yes, I must stop making myself late for my own life by stopping focusing on somebody else's life.
No this is not right and it is because of you Lord that I can now see the light.

Lord your word is a lamp unto my feet and a light unto my path.
I will no longer focus on the math of, "why did they have to say this," or "why did they have to do that."

I will counteract it by displaying love, by offering hope, yes, I will learn to cope by allowing you to destroy this yoke.
Up until this point, the enemy has been tearing up the joint of my mind.

Having me concentrating on trying to make a point inadvertently trying to be conjoint with the world.
Forgetting that I am no longer a part of the world.

I will not think of the positive things like I attend the conventions once annually.
I will think of positive things daily like it is a way of living.

I will not speak positivity out of something said that is clever or witty.
I will speak positivity out of spiritual clarity.

I will continue to bury me and allow the new me to break forth thoroughly and remember you'll never leave me, though the enemies job is to deceive me.

I will be kind and speak peaceably though my flesh would like to give them a piece of me.
I will display what you displayed on Calvary by loving others unselfishly and letting go of me to love you wholly.

DEVOTION

God gave us individual aspirations and goals for us to fulfill our mission. We cannot successfully complete our mission if we are busy focusing on negativity. For, it is a hindrance and a tactic of the enemy to prohibit us from spiritually growing and to lure our hearts away from God. This is a part of why the Bible instructs us to think on: "whatsoever things are true, whatsoever things are honest, whatsoever things are just, whatsoever things are pure, whatsoever things are lovely, whatsoever things are of good report; if there be any virtue, and if there be any praise, think on these things" (Phil. 4:8).

When we focus on the way that the person(s) have mistreated or offended us, we create issues. The enemy sows the seed, but it is up to us whether or not we allow it to take root. The Bible lets us know that he is going to shoot darts, but if we have the shield of faith on, it will not be able to enter our spirits. We have to realize that the devil is fighting to separate us from the love of God.

If we love God with our whole heart and mind, we will only focus on Him and our actions will display these thoughts. Thus, we will be outwardly magnifying Him. Focusing on God's love and His word aligns us with Him to the extent that we begin walking in His judgments and statutes. As we continue on the walk, we become less and less concerned with things such as evening the score with our opposers. We have to pray and be continually led by God so that we will only operate in the Spirit. "This I say then, walk in the Spirit, and ye shall not fulfill the lust of the flesh" (Galatians 5:16).

QUESTIONS TO PONDER

1. What has been occupying your attention lately?

2. If the enemy has trapped you into thinking more negatively than positively, use the above devotional to write out ways you can combat these negative thoughts from controlling your mind.

DAY 10
I WILL PRAISE HIM

I will praise Him, everywhere He sends me!
I will praise Him, even if it causes jealousy and envy!
I will praise Him with every gift that's in me!

No, I'm not just talking.
These are the things I am exhibiting in my daily walking, by declining the invitation of what the enemy is offering.

I will praise Him! Even though the world is constantly trying to erase Him.
I will praise Him! Because He raised me and though the weapons were formed none of them have even been able to graze me!

I will praise Him!
It does not matter who it offends.

No, I won't tease Him with no little, "hallelujah" and "thank you Jesus," but I will praise Him!
Because I could've had 4 & 5 different baby fathers.

He could've allowed me to go farther and farther away from His loving hand or even cave under the pressure of all of life's demands!

Even if you do have 4 & 5 baby fathers, God is able to take you farther than the one that never left his cleft and He'd still would be operating in complete righteousness.

You see right just then,
I probably irritated somebody.
His ways are not our ways and His thoughts are not our thoughts and oughts are not in his heart.

I will praise Him. You too, after all you've been through have something to praise Him for.
We all have something to praise Him for.

I will praise Him!

DEVOTION

Praise is a requirement that is not only for the Christian believer, but it is a commandment for everyone. The Bible says: "Let everything that hath breath praise the LORD" (Psa. 150:6). If God has graced you with gifts and talents, you must praise Him with all of them. "For unto whomsoever much is given, of him shall be much required" (Luke 12:48). Utilizing your gifts and talents may generate jealousy from others, but you must be strong and praise God despite their feelings.

God did not inquire with them about giving you the talent and He does not need permission to use any vessel. He said, "Behold, all souls are mine" (Ezek. 18:4). Furthermore: "The earth is the LORD's, and the fullness thereof; the world, and they that dwell therein" (Psa. 24:1). God alone is the orchestrator, thus, He gives as He sees fit. Be forbearing of the saint or individual who despises your gifts, pray for strength and continue to use it, increase it and perfect it.

QUESTIONS TO PONDER

1. Are you giving God your best praise? Have you been minimizing your gifts to fit the mold that others believe you should fit in? Journal about any gifts you have not completely surrendered over to God and work on relinquishing your will for His.

2. Are you utilizing all of your gifts and talents to praise Him? If not, write out different ways you can begin to use and enhance them.

DAY 11

FAILURE

I experienced such gigantic failure that left me with feelings of melancholy that only Mahalia Jackson could project!
I felt like such a reject.

Now when I take time to reflect on the past, I see that all the overcast was sent to present what was meant.
See, I thought that my story had the have the same blueprinted glory as other success stories.

The thought eluded me that God wanted to do something for me that would be extraordinary.
See, by faith I can say that I will experience such victory
that will go down in history.
Because I have sought God who will unlock the mystery.

See, my drought filled the gap between my past and destiny.
The feelings of battery was to keep me in contact with humanity.
Before honor comes humility.
So, these afflictions allowed me to sustain my mobility, and not allow my abilities to clog any vicinity.

So, I would still have agility.
For it was through my failure that I conquered what was unheard.
When I thought that my mind would leave,
God showed me it was Christmas Eve.

When I felt like a coward God, told me I was something like a tower.
That's still hard for me to believe up until this very hour.
But I forget that He said that we'd be endowed with power.
So, it's not coming out of our strength.

He also said,
"For I know the thoughts that I think towards you thoughts of peace to give you an expected in."
You can win, when you get this idea within, that, "I am able to flip the script."
Just when it looks like the enemy will rip you to shreds I will perform what I said.

"There is nothing that can stop me from multiplying thee,
from fortifying thee, all those who are in me don't have to be concerned with what the enemy has learned or is plotting. Though they are shining now, they will soon be rotting."

All that they seemed to have been blocking, God will begin unlocking before them, in such a way that they won't be able to ignore Him. "The more you ignore them, the more you'll continue to soar past them inevitably outlast them, all the way over into life everlasting. Just continue casting your cares upon me and I will bring there calamity suddenly."

DEVOTION

Sometimes life's ups and downs can make us feel like God got something wrong. Usually, it is the place where we feel like there is an error that pushes us to our true purpose. My failures and grief led me to write pieces of poetry that have been therapeutic for myself and others. If I did not experience the pain or embarrassment, I would not have realized my potential.

Some tests that we go through are to help someone else when they experience the same test later. We must be open enough to birth purpose. Unfortunately, greatness does not just manifest it is produced through tribulation. The tribulation may include embarrassment, mistreatment, rejection, and so many other undesirable experiences. However, we must be encouraged with the belief that, "all things work together for good to them that love God

QUESTIONS TO PONDER

1. Have you recently taken a blow of rejection that has left you questioning your purpose? If so, did you seek God to see if this was His will for your life? If you did seek him, what do you think the purpose was for this experience?

2. Take advantage of this feeling and use it for your good. Seek God for guidance and write down the ideas that He reveals.

DAY 12

WOMEN

Women who are purpose driven.
Women who have completely given their lives to God.
Women who are not afraid to dig deep into the word of God.
Women who are not afraid to face the odds.
Women who are not afraid to pray and wail in a time of travail.
Women who will not allow their passion for God to go stale,
but will keep it freshly maintained like we keep our hair.
Women who are living righteously.
Women who have forsaken living riotously.
Women who are walking in sobriety.

The Bible doesn't say for us to walk in a variety of ways.
It says, "teach us to number our days."
Women who are worthy of that knight and shining armor.
Yes, we climb on chairs and look upstairs trying to see if God is there and if He hears our prayers, but are we prepared?
Or are we opposing the Word of God by focusing on ideas like, "God isn't fair?"

See we have this perspective, because we're not in line.

No, we're not in tune with his Spirit.

We are so far off we think it's December when we're in June.

We should be cleaning up our homes, sweeping out our rooms, and saturating our hearts with sweet perfume in preparation of the bridegroom.

Because ladies it's almost midnight, for the hands on the clock have long since passed noon.

DEVOTION

It is easy to ask for things without considering what they cost. It is important for us to understand who we are and what our purpose is. The Bible talks about the virtuous woman and how she is clothed with honor and strength. This honor is a reflection of her character. It is imperative for us to have good characteristics. If we possess the attributes of the virtuous woman, we will be trustworthy. We should not ask God for things we are not preparing for. Therefore, we must pray and work diligently toward them while petitioning God for them. We must also take heed to God's word. If we do not follow His instructions, we will be devoid of the strength that the blessing will require and we will need this strength in order to fulfill the perfect will of God in our lives.

By taking heed to the word of God, we are exercising ourselves in His word. The more that we practice this, the more we will display godly characteristics. We have to walk in the Spirit to avoid walking in the flesh. This has to be done diligently and intentionally. Thus, we cannot give our flesh sabbaticals; we have to continually deny it of its ungodly desires. Though, not all of our fleshly desires are ungodly. For example, having a sexual desire for the opposite sex is not ungodly, it is natural, however, it can only be done lawfully within the confines of marriage. If we are not married, we must deny our flesh this privilege until we become married.

QUESTIONS TO PONDER

1. How is your character? This is your personal devotion, so be honest with yourself. Are you producing the fruit of the Spirit or the works of the flesh?

2. Have you previously examined your character? Have you been working towards changing the things that you are aware are not pleasing to God? If not, use the above devotion to map out a way to begin correcting these issues.

DAY 13

FLY

How canst I fly with life's burdens weighing upon me like an eye with a sty. Should I just lay here and die?
No wait I can fly.
For it is my father who resides in the sky.

So, even if the pain doesn't immediately subside.
I shall continually strive, until I can effortlessly glide.
This isn't pride, but what you hear is my tenacity to reach my full capacity. You see the devil has been relentlessly after me.

Though ironically, adversity makes me thirsty.
Who but God could make tribulation affect one reversely.
So, I'll continue to rehearse the manual, till I become such a spiritual geek that I grievously reek of your ways of meekness.

Till I no longer reflect the former days.
Till I only reflect your Son you gave.
Till I reject every ungodly crave.
No, I'm not just talking about the usual subjects, such as: sex, us human beings are far more complex.

I'm talking about walking in complete righteousness.
You see just because you left the devil doesn't mean that all of his stuff has left you.
There is a process that we all must go through.
We got daddy issues, mama issues, gossip issues, lazy issues, crazy issues!

No, this was not written to be used as an excuse to keep anyone in a spiritual noose.
Rather to stop you from drowning in your spiritual overthinking that you're sinking when you're actually spiritually shrinking.
So, even with feelings of timidity as high as a Summer's day humidity,
I shall expand these wings and fly.

DEVOTION

As a Christian believer, the growth process can sometimes be frustrating. At times we may think that we have reached a mark that we have not. God reveals these things, during the testing process. When He tests us, we can see where we are in him. Sometimes, the failure of the test makes us feel inadequate and devastated, but we must continue to trust that our perseverance will get us to our expected end.

God is our friend and He is working to put us back together as we were in the beginning. Consequently, we do not have to worry or fret. We just have to work diligently to get to the level that He requires of us in each season and not take advantage of his grace. During this process, we can rest in the fact that "all things work together for the good to them who are called according to his purpose" (Rom. 8:28). God does all things well and He does not start a thing without finishing it, as indicated in this scripture: "Being confident of this very thing, that He who has begun in you a good work will perform it unto the day of Jesus Christ" (Phil. 1:6).

QUESTIONS TO PONDER

1. Consider where you are currently in your walk with Christ and write out ways that you can better your relationship with God. Are you allowing God to elevate you seasonally or are you delaying your growth by drawing back?

2. Are you feeling discouraged because you desire to be at a higher level in Christ? Journal these thoughts and be encouraged by the above devotion.

DAY 14
PACKAGE

Do you ever feel like you just want to disappear? Not for an entire year, but just for this situation right here? This is the route on which the blessing is being delivered. Don't you sometimes wish you could overnight it and instruct the angels to deliver it with care?

Like yes, don't hurt me right there and yes that is where I would like you to land it right where I planned it. Yup, possibly around the age of 32. Lord, I want you to do what you said you would do 10 years ago. So, I'm going to expect it because I projected that it had to happen around this time. Because that's when some friends of mine received there's.

So forgive me for being anxious, but they got theirs. See comparison will have you sitting somewhere with a heart full of sin.
You're dwelling on somebody else's blessing when you could lessen the blow of not knowing when, by occupying, by serving Him and learning Him.

Yes, you could ease your pain by being prayerful and being there for other people, not worrying about if they can do something for you that will equal up to what you did for them.
Work on honoring Him!

For the word says that: "if we delight ourselves in you, you would give us the desires of our heart."
So, let's not try to pick the word apart to see if we can cause God to have a change of heart.

Instead, re-route our direction and start to follow Jesus' directions.
For, then we will end up at the right intersection at the right time, to fall in line with the flow of traffic.
We will not have to worry about an unforeseen collision because God will have already made provision.

You also said that He who hungers and thirst after righteousness shall be filled which means we are not supposed to be hungry and thirsty for the carnal things more than the eternal things.
We have to be focused on whether or not you are pleased and not somebody purchasing us a ring.

DEVOTION

Everyone has goals; however, our expectation and God's timing do not always coincide. This is a prevalent issue amongst single women and society exacerbates it. However, as Christians, our lives are in Christ and He knows what is best for us. Just like when you were a kid and you wanted to attend an event at that friends house and your parents said "no". The "no" was for your protection; not to stop you from having fun.

When God gives us provision, He does the exact same thing as our parents. He protects us! Some petitions that we have placed before God, we are not ready to receive. Other unanswered prayers are so that He can get all of the glory when He does answer. Some individuals are set aside for God only and will not marry. There are multiple reasons that are beyond what we can conceive; however, God is omniscient. Therefore, we can exchange our limited understanding for his complete understanding. This is why it is important for us Christians to be content and to set our desires on heavenly things. For, our feet will inevitably follow the steps of our heart.

QUESTIONS TO PONDER

1. What is your focus in life? Are you worried about becoming a wife? If you are a male, are you worried about finding a wife? If so, using the above devotional write down ways that you believe could better your perspective during your wait.

2. Are you adding to your talents and your faith? If not, write short term and long term goals to help you increase your gift.

DAY 15

FIRE WITHIN

It'll be like fire when you go higher.
Some things won't even touch the tire of your situation because God will solely be your motivation.
He will have given you so much patience and you'll be consistently waiting for him with the right spirit within.
This is the result of one having forsaken dwindling in sin and you'll then be ready to win and going higher again.

The enemy will be mad because He will no longer see that sad soul.
Then you'll be on the verge of pure gold with this love that its depths are untold.
Watch me unfold and give you as much as you can hold.
You will be on the verge of exploding because your soul will be overloaded with my spiritual gift.
Gifts will I reveal to you that you didn't know were in you.
I'mma send you from venue to venue, from stage to stage, and from page to page.
You'll just get better with age.
I'mma give you a platform, but it's for my people for you to warn.

DEVOTION

Being born again of the water and of the Spirit is mandatory for one to enter into the kingdom of Heaven. The more you walk with God and truly live for him the more you will grow and resemble him. Your walk with God should involve praying, fasting, reading the bible and faithfully attending a church that teaches The Word of God. The manifestation of this growth will be more anointing, more understanding of His Word, more love and more self-denial. This transformation will lead to God being able to enlarge your territory.

The enlargement of one's territory can be through one's gifts and talents, "A man's gift maketh room for him and bringeth him before great men" (Prov. 18:16). If the Christian believer willingly serves and walks with God, He grants this believer their hearts desires, "Delight thyself also in the LORD: and He shall give thee the desires of thine heart" (Psalm. 37:4). It is very important to understand that not every promise formulates overnight, it is a process. This process requires steps which ultimately produce the final outcome. This means that we should not be so focused on the grandeur end, but journey on and believe God for that end. This requires patience and an obedient spirit. Remember not to despise the day of small beginnings (Zechariah 4:10).

Note: When considering versions of the Bible to add to your library, The King James Version is a good way to receive the word, for, it is the closest translation to the original Hebrew and Greek language it was written in.

QUESTIONS TO PONDER

1. Have you been born again of the water and of the spirit? If not, Acts 2:38 of the Bible, provides instructions on what you must do to be saved. If you already have been born again of the water and spirit, are you still on fire for God?

2. Consider your relationship with God and see if there are areas where you need to surrender to the Lord and journal ways to begin relinquishing your will over to Him.

THANK YOU!
LIST OF SPONSORS

This page is dedicated to those who purchased a book bundle to make the publishing of this project possible. Also listed are the business sponsors who advertised in this book.

$50 Sponsorship	Business Sponsors
Anthony Abraham Jr.	Letia Hardy
Angela Cato	Nekia Harvey
Taniesha Dingle	Dwayne Fisher
Rufus Hilton	Diane Palmer
Eric McNair	Ebony Harris
Martha Powell	Jackie James
Christina Saunders	
Gwendolynn Simmons	
Jason Upshaw	
Linda Hope	

SUPPORT MY BUSINESS SPONSORS

COME AND SHOP WITH DIANE!
SOMETHING FOR EVERYONE!

GO TO YOURAVON.COM/CATHERINEPALMER

OR CALL ME, YOUR LOCAL AVON AGENT @

667-210-7193

BIG PICTURE CONTRACTING
LICENSED IN MARYLAND

EMAIL: ZEC4N6@AOL.COM

SERVICES INCLUDE: COMMERCIAL PAINTING, CONSTRUCTION, AND LEAD INSPECTION SERVICES.

443-473-0823

"Starting my Paparazzi Accessories business allowed me to stay at home with my son after he was diagnosed with a disability. I am now the CEO of Virtuous Glam and Jewels by Nekia LLC." Whether you are looking to supplement your income, to build an empire of your own, or to shop our fabulous $5 fashion, it is possible with Paparazzi Accessories.

Shop new releases daily!

Contact me or visit my website to start your business today!

VirtuousGlamAndJewelsbyNekiaLLC.Com   (443) 430-5029

SHOP NOW

BENEFITS
- Work From Home!
- Be Your Own Boss!
- 45% Commission!
- Flexible Hours!
- Unlimited Earning Potential!

EARN FREE JEWELRY

Your pain has a purpose. "To God Be All The Glory" on sale now!

More than poetry, it's ministry!

"Your trials not only make you strong, it gives you strength to strengthen another. Bits of Poetry, Spoken Word is a collection of poems written to edify the mind. (Poetry for young women)

AlmaFisher.Com

As Christian authors we write like our readers lives depend on it, because it does.

Accepting submissions:
bepublishingco.com

How To Keep Them Reading
A guide to writing an engaging book.

Are you struggling to finish your book? Get the help you need today!

On Sale now **$24.99**

www.bepublishingco.com

BE PUBLISHING CO. OFFERS ONLINE WRITING COURSES

Writing is a skill that anyone can acquire. Take courses from home. Some courses have a waiting list. Make sure you get on it before it closes.

JOIN THE JOURNEY

LIFETOWORDS.COM

The Fisher Girls new release "Full Attention" is available now on all digital platforms and they are available for interviews! @thefishergirls

Facebook https://www.facebook.com/thefishergirls/
Instagram https://instagram.com/thefishergirls
Twitter https://twitter.com/@thefisher_girls

Did you get our new single? It'll make you move!

THANK YOU SO MUCH FOR YOUR SUPPORT

HELP ME MAKE THIS A BEST SELLER CONSIDER PURCHASING ONE FOR A FRIEND.

www.ingramcontent.com/pod-product-compliance
Lightning Source LLC
Chambersburg PA
CBHW072038110526
44592CB00012B/1462